Alfred's Basic Piano Library
Duet Book • Level 4

Selected and Edited by E. L. Lancaster & Morton Manus

The pleasure young students get from adding popular music to their piano lessons has been well documented. The positive reaction we received from teachers following the introduction of Alfred's *Top Hits Solo Books* (Levels 1B–4) and *Top Hits Christmas Books* (Levels 1B–4) has been overwhelming. We are now pleased to add *Duet Books* (Levels 1B–4) to the *Top Hits* series.

Playing duets is important to the musical growth of the young pianist. Duets aid with the development of steady rhythm, listening for proper balance, and playing with appropriate dynamics. Finally, working together in a collaborative performance teaches more than just music. Not only does this duet series contain some of the most popular music ever written, but the arrangements are unique in a number of ways:

- The primo and secondo are equal in difficulty, with the melody distributed between both parts.
- Students are aided in achieving the correct balance between melody and accompaniment by dynamic signs and the inclusion of the lyrics with the melody only.
- Careful consideration has been given to spacing the music so that page turns are easy; measure numbers have been included for reference during practice sessions.

This book is correlated page-by-page with Lesson Book 4 of Alfred's Basic Piano Library; pieces should be assigned based on the instructions in the upper-right corner of each title page. Since the melodies and rhythms of popular music do not always lend themselves to precise grading, you may find that these pieces are sometimes a little more difficult than the corresponding pages in the Lesson Book. The teacher's judgment is the most important factor in deciding when to begin each title.

When the books in the *Top Hits* series (Solo, Christmas, Duet) are assigned in conjunction with the Lesson Books, these appealing pieces reinforce new concepts as they are introduced. In addition, the motivation from the music increases student interest in piano study to successively higher levels.

All I Ask of You (Arr. by Dennis Alexander)
from THE PHANTOM OF THE OPERA 26

Chariots of Fire (Arr. by Tom Gerou)
from CHARIOTS OF FIRE 32

Climb Ev'ry Mountain (Arr. by Catherine Rollin)
from THE SOUND OF MUSIC 8

Eleanor Rigby (Arr. by Tom Gerou) 22

God Help the Outcasts
(Arr. by George Peter Tingley)
from Walt Disney's THE HUNCHBACK OF NOTRE DAME . 42

My Heart Will Go On (Love Theme from 'Titanic')
(Arr. by Martha Mier)
from the Paramount and Twentieth Century Fox Motion Picture TITANIC 2

Rockin' Robin (Arr. by Margaret Goldston) 16

Splish Splash (Arr. by George Peter Tingley) 38

Y.M.C.A. (Arr. by Sharon Aaronson) 12

Published by

Distributed by
Alfred Publishing Co., Inc.

ISBN 0-7390-0837-4
All Rights Reserved. Printed in USA.

Cover photos: Camera, popcorn box © 1999 PhotoDisc, Inc.
Backgrounds, movie clapboard © Eyewire, Inc.

My Heart Will Go On
(Love Theme from 'Titanic')
from the Paramount and Twentieth Century Fox Motion Picture TITANIC

Use with Alfred's Basic Piano Library,
LESSON BOOK 4, after page 7.

Secondo

Music by James Horner
Lyric by Will Jennings
Arr. by Martha Mier

Moderato

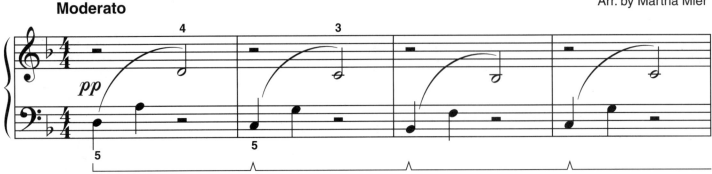

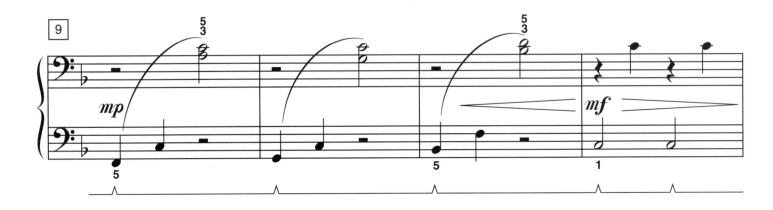

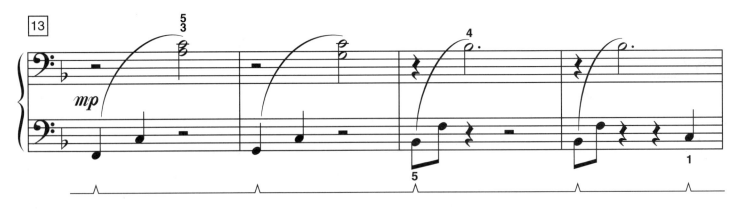

Copyright © 1997 by Famous Music Corporation, Ensign Music Corporation, TCF Music Publishing, Inc., Fox Film Music Corporation and Blue Sky Rider Songs
All Rights for Blue Sky Rider Songs Administered by Irving Music, Inc.
International Copyright Secured   All Rights Reserved

My Heart Will Go On
(Love Theme from 'Titanic')

from the Paramount and Twentieth Century Fox Motion Picture TITANIC

Use with Alfred's Basic Piano Library,
LESSON BOOK 4, after page 7.

Primo

Music by James Horner
Lyric by Will Jennings
Arr. by Martha Mier

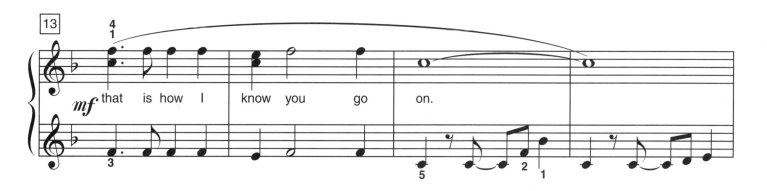

Copyright © 1997 by Famous Music Corporation, Ensign Music Corporation, TCF Music Publishing, Inc., Fox Film Music Corporation and Blue Sky Rider Songs
All Rights for Blue Sky Rider Songs Administered by Irving Music, Inc.
International Copyright Secured   All Rights Reserved

My Heart Will Go On
Secondo

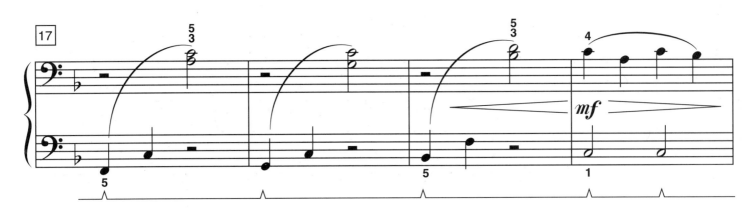
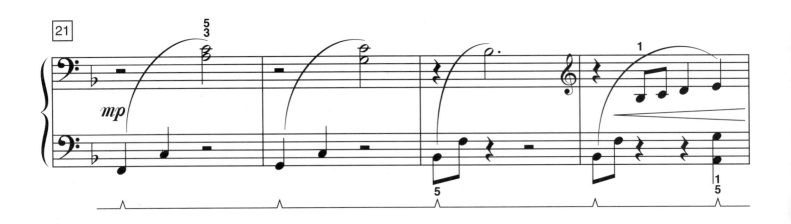
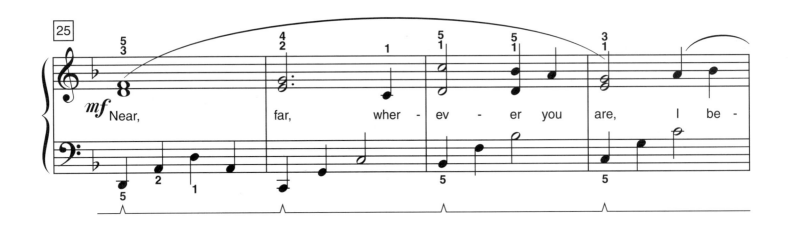
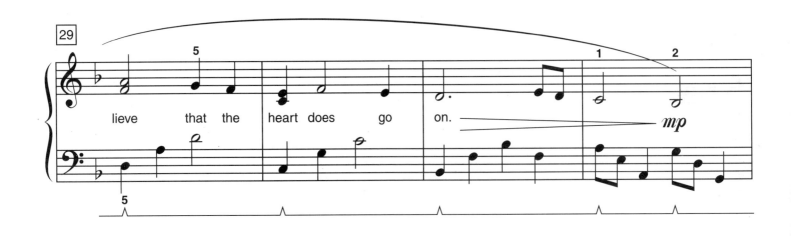

My Heart Will Go On
Primo

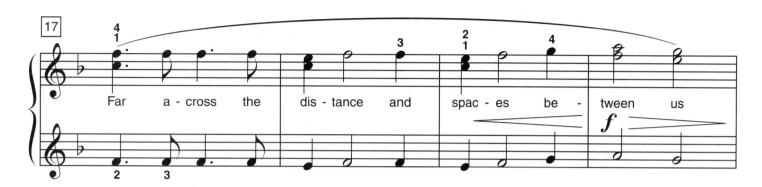
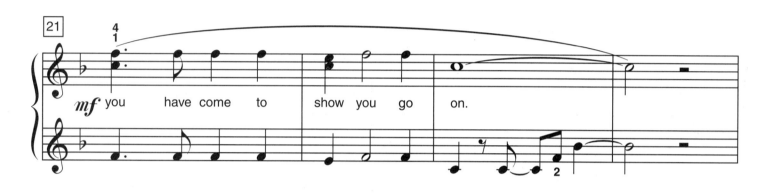
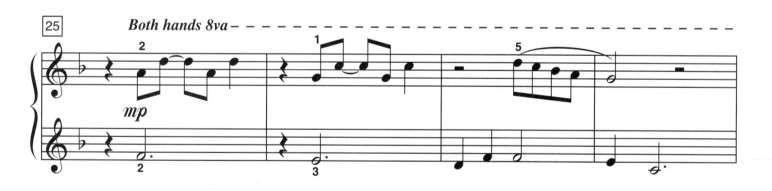
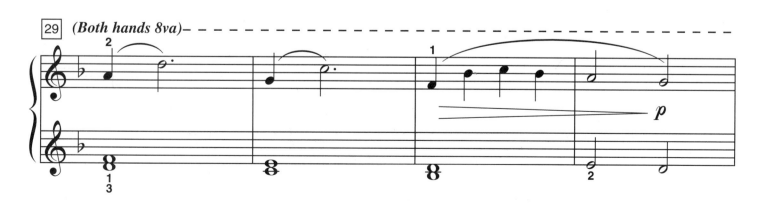

My Heart Will Go On
Secondo

My Heart Will Go On
Primo

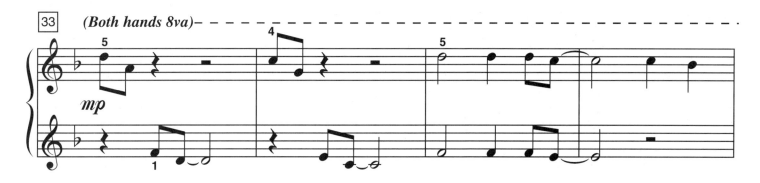
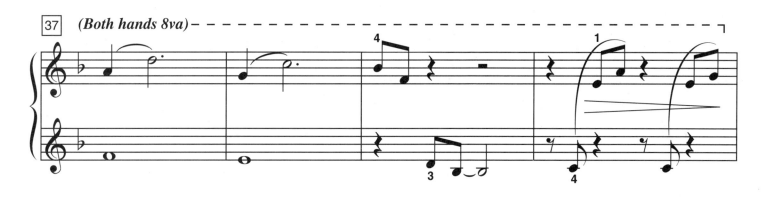

Climb Ev'ry Mountain
from THE SOUND OF MUSIC

Primo

Lyrics by Oscar Hammerstein II
Music by Richard Rodgers
Arr. by Catherine Rollin

Use after page 11.

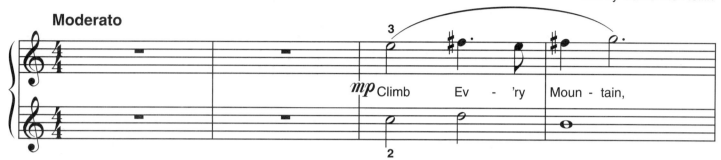
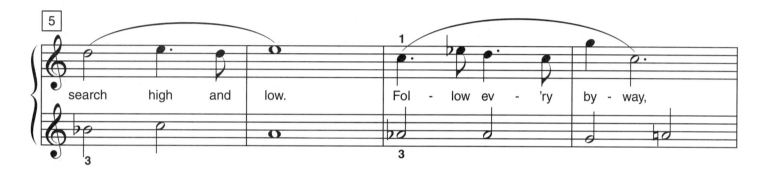
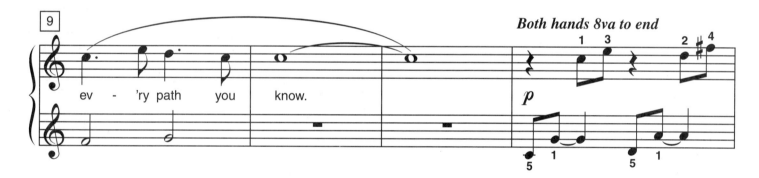

Copyright © 1959 by Richard Rodgers and Oscar Hammerstein II
Copyright Renewed
WILLIAMSON MUSIC owner of publication and allied rights throughout the world
International Copyright Secured   All Rights Reserved

Climb Ev'ry Mountain
Secondo

Climb Ev'ry Mountain
Primo

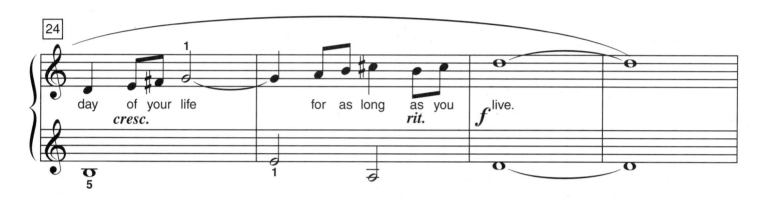
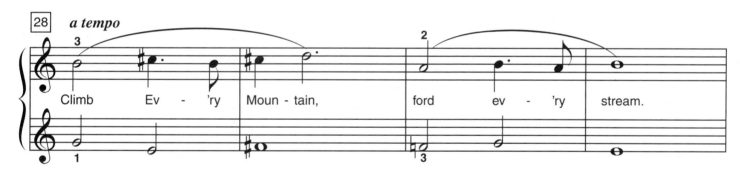
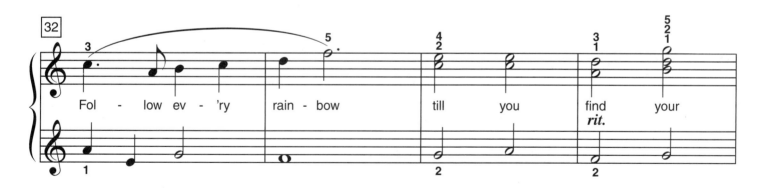

Y.M.C.A.
Secondo

Y.M.C.A.
Primo

Rockin' Robin

Secondo

Words and Music by J. Thomas
Arr. by Margaret Goldston

Use after page 23.

*Optional: Play pairs of eighth notes a bit unevenly, long-short.

©1958 Recordo Music Publishers
Copyright Renewed
All Rights Reserved

Rockin' Robin
Secondo

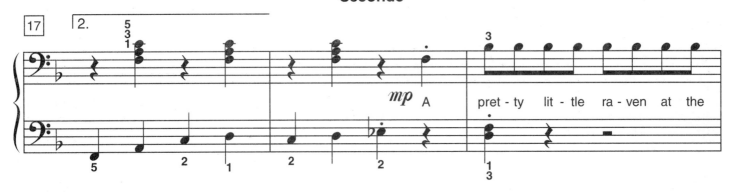
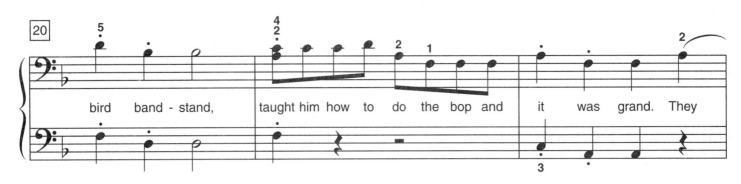

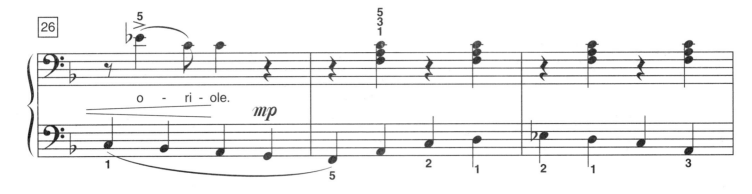

Rockin' Robin
Primo

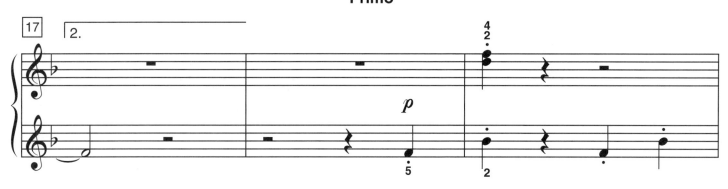
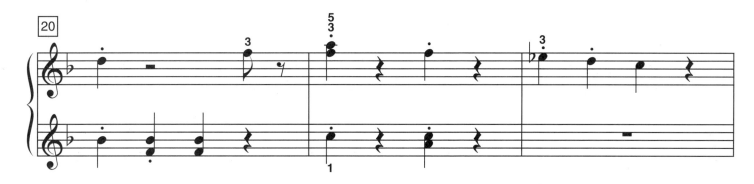

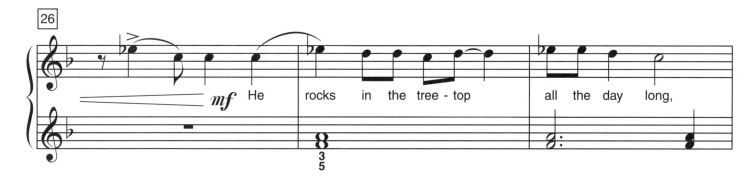
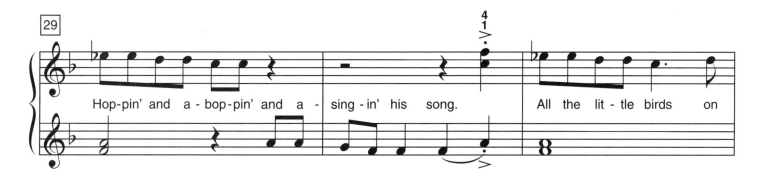

Rockin' Robin
Secondo

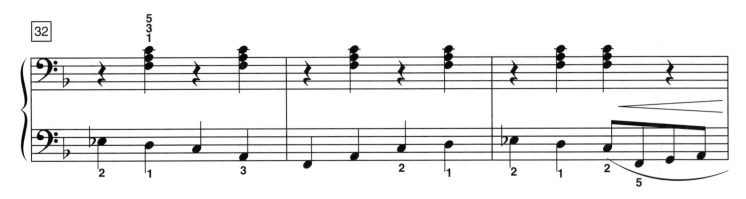
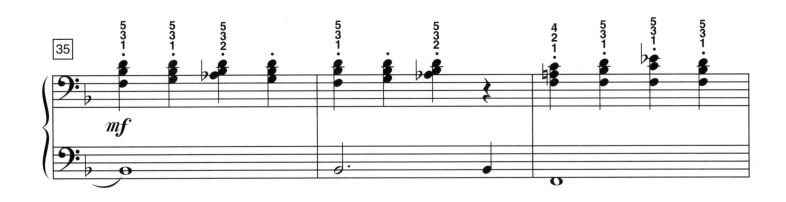
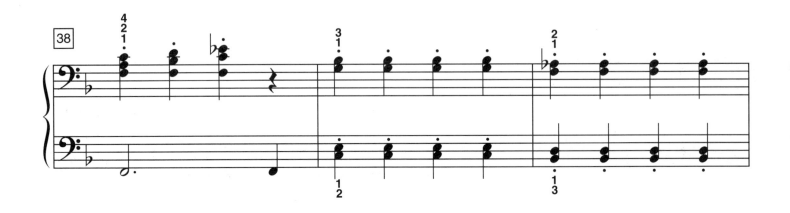
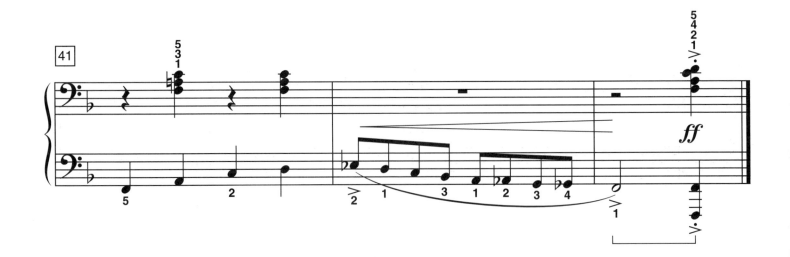

Rockin' Robin
Primo

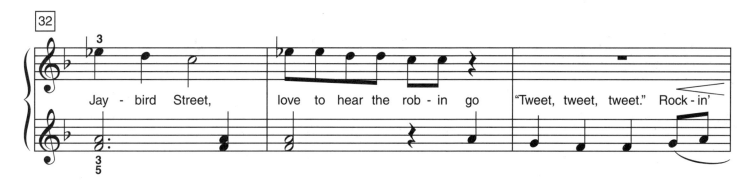
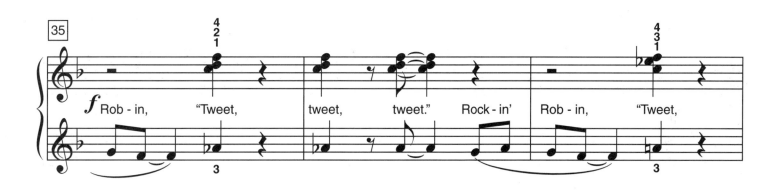
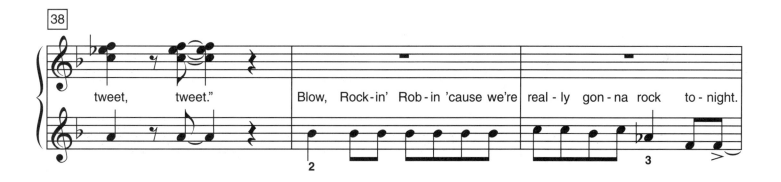
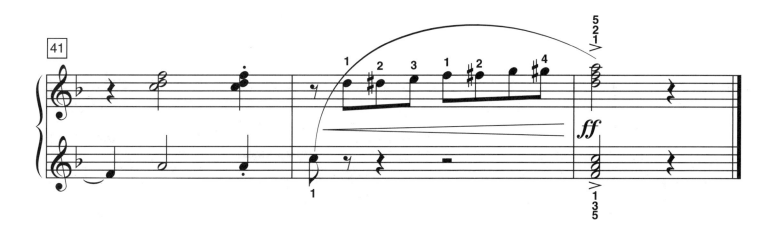

Eleanor Rigby
Secondo

Use after page 29.

Words and Music by
John Lennon and Paul McCartney
Arr. by Tom Gerou

Allegro moderato

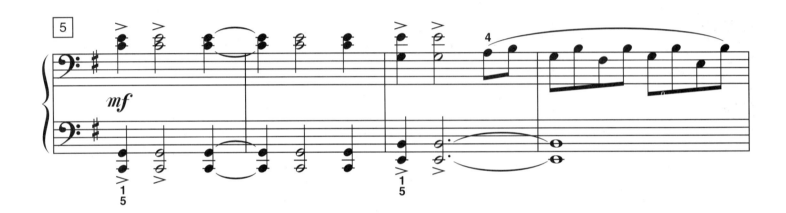

Copyright © 1966 Sony/ATV Songs LLC
Copyright Renewed
All Rights Administered by Sony/ATV Music Publishing, 8 Music Square West, Nashville, TN 37203
International Copyright Secured   All Rights Reserved

Eleanor Rigby
Primo

Words and Music by
John Lennon and Paul McCartney
Arr. by Tom Gerou

Allegro moderato
Both hands 8va throughout

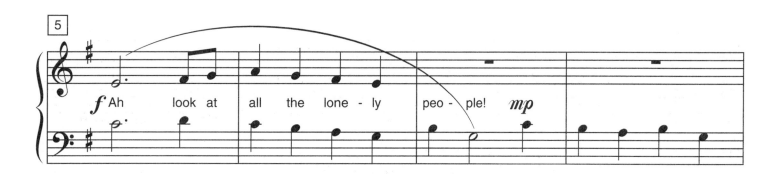
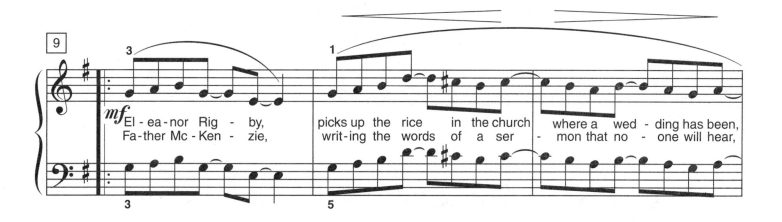
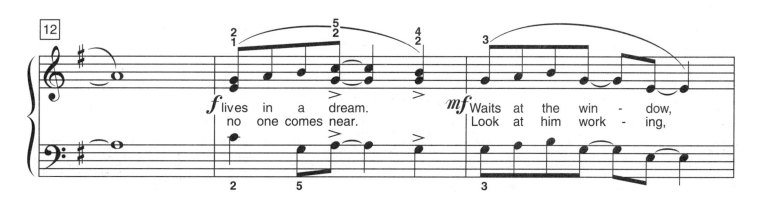

Eleanor Rigby
Secondo

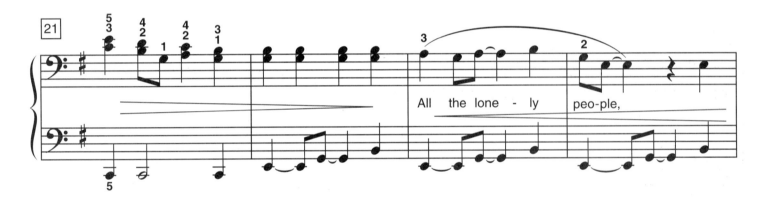

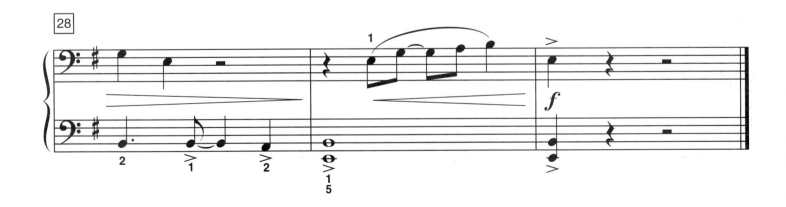

Eleanor Rigby
Primo

All I Ask of You
from THE PHANTOM OF THE OPERA

Primo

Music by Andrew Lloyd Webber
Lyrics by Charles Hart
Additional Lyrics by Richard Stilgoe
Arr. by Dennis Alexander

Use after page 35.

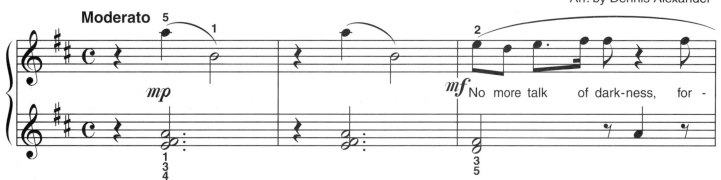

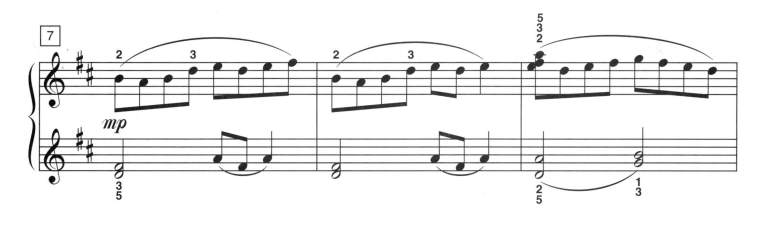

© Copyright 1986 The Really Useful Group Ltd.
All Rights for the United States and Canada Administered by PolyGram International Publishing, Inc.
International Copyright Secured   All Rights Reserved

All I Ask of You
Secondo

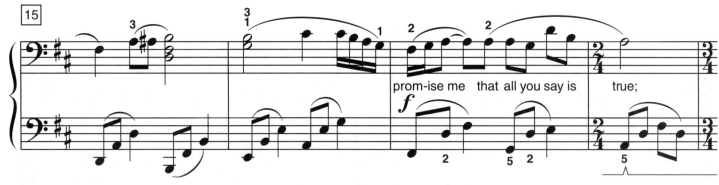
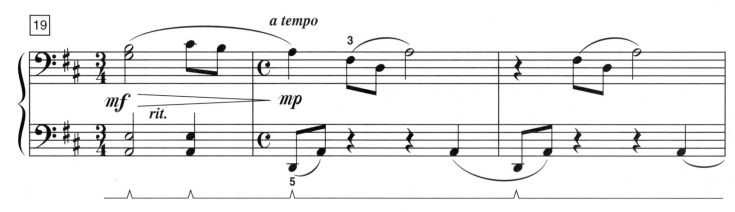

All I Ask of You
Secondo

All I Ask of You
Primo

Chariots of Fire

from CHARIOTS OF FIRE

Secondo

Use after page 35.

Music by Vangelis
Arr. by Tom Gerou

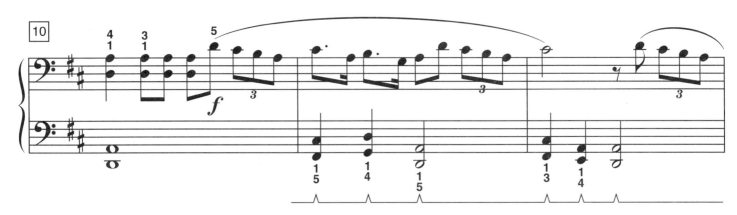

© 1981 EMI MUSIC PUBLISHING LTD.
All Rights for the World, excluding Holland, Controlled and Administered by EMI APRIL MUSIC INC.
All Rights Reserved   International Copyright Secured   Used by Permission

Chariots of Fire

from CHARIOTS OF FIRE

Primo

Music by Vangelis
Arr. by Tom Gerou

Use after page 35.

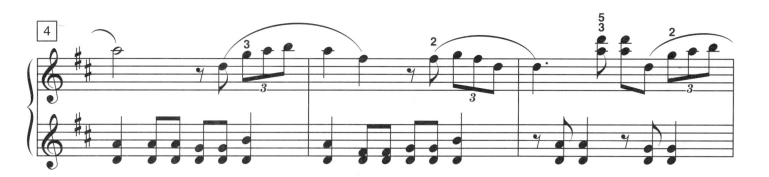
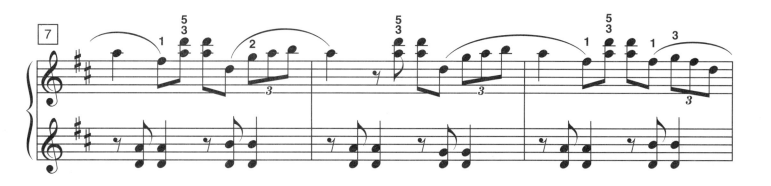
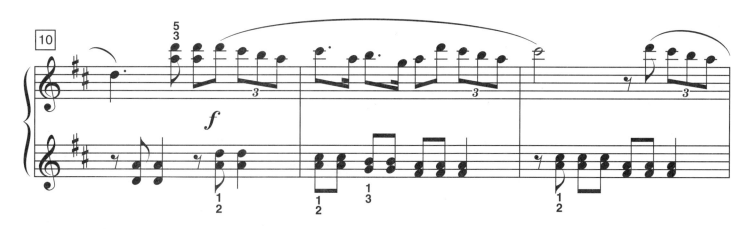

© 1981 EMI MUSIC PUBLISHING LTD.
All Rights for the World, excluding Holland, Controlled and Administered by EMI APRIL MUSIC INC.
All Rights Reserved   International Copyright Secured   Used by Permission

Chariots of Fire
Secondo

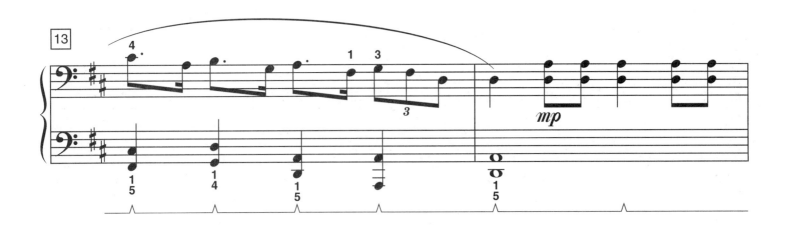
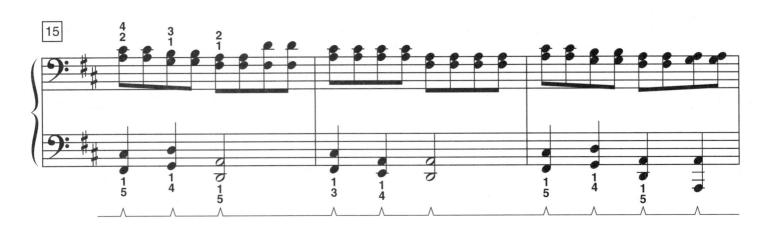

Chariots of Fire
Primo

Chariots of Fire
Secondo

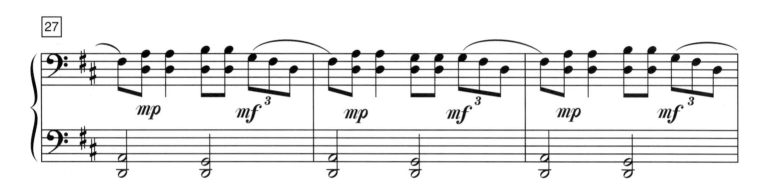

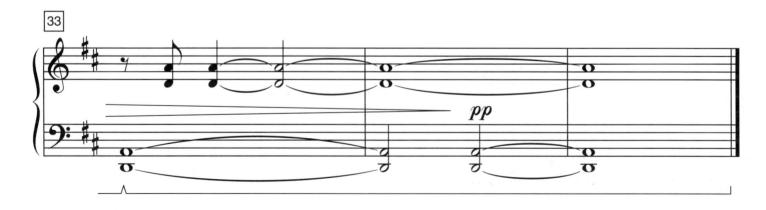

Chariots of Fire
Primo

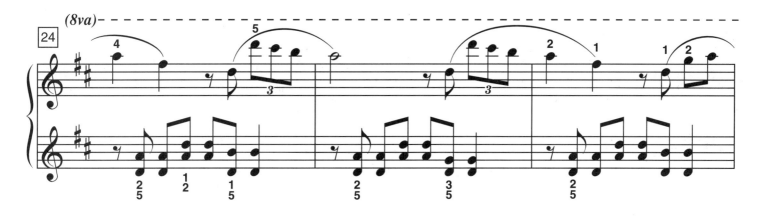

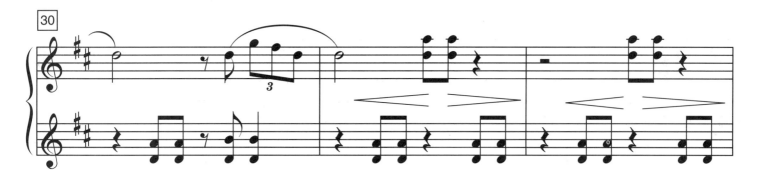

Splish Splash
Secondo

Use after page 39.

Words and Music by
Bobby Darin and Murray Kaufman
Arr. by George Peter Tingley

Splish Splash
Secondo

Splish Splash
Primo

God Help the Outcasts
from Walt Disney's THE HUNCHBACK OF NOTRE DAME

Use after page 47.

Secondo

Music by Alan Menken
Lyrics by Stephen Schwartz
Arr. by George Peter Tingley

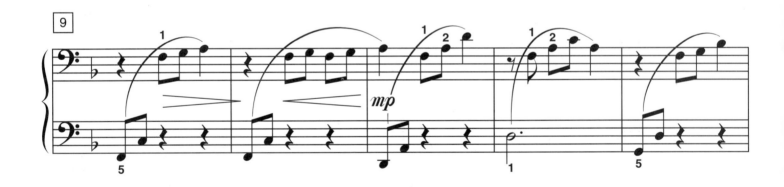

© 1996 Wonderland Music Company, Inc. and Walt Disney Music Company
All Rights Reserved   Used by Permission

God Help the Outcasts
from Walt Disney's THE HUNCHBACK OF NOTRE DAME

Primo

Music by Alan Menken
Lyrics by Stephen Schwartz
Arr. by George Peter Tingley

Use after page 47.

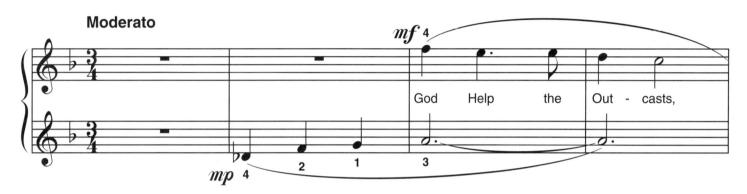

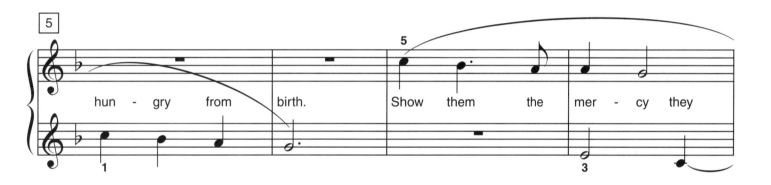

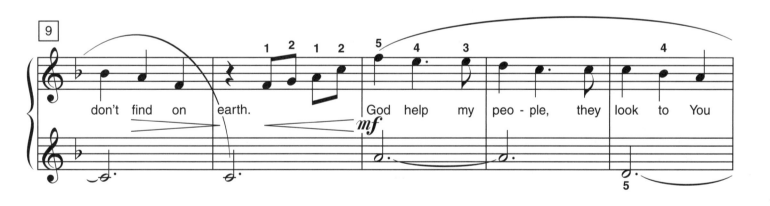

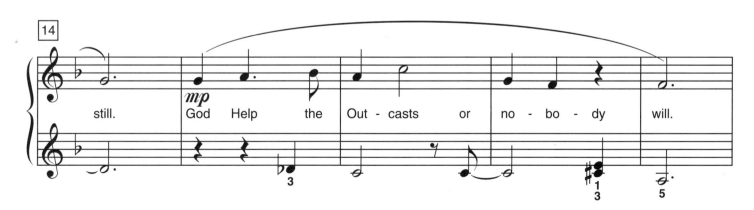

© 1996 Wonderland Music Company, Inc. and Walt Disney Music Company
All Rights Reserved   Used by Permission

God Help the Outcasts
Secondo

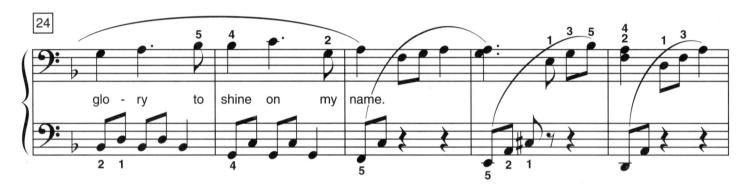
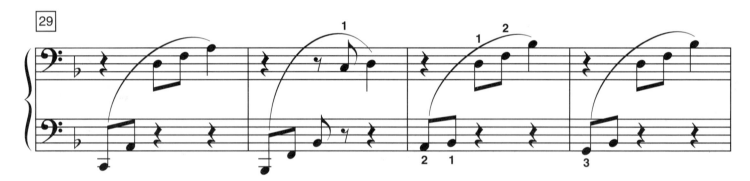
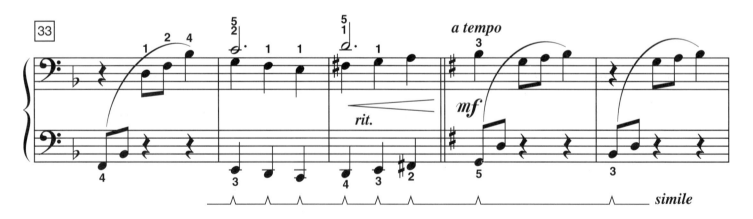
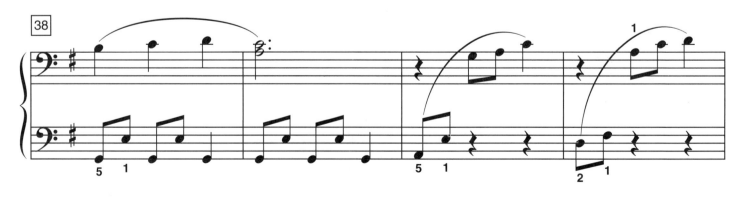

God Help the Outcasts
Primo

God Help the Outcasts
Secondo

God Help the Outcasts
Primo

NEW!

Alfred's Basic Piano Library
TOP HITS!
SOLO BOOKS LEVELS 1B–4

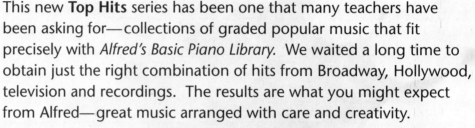

This new **Top Hits** series has been one that many teachers have been asking for—collections of graded popular music that fit precisely with *Alfred's Basic Piano Library*. We waited a long time to obtain just the right combination of hits from Broadway, Hollywood, television and recordings. The results are what you might expect from Alfred—great music arranged with care and creativity.

The arrangers selected for this series include Sharon Aaronson, Dennis Alexander, Christine H. Barden, Tom Gerou, Martha Mier and George Peter Tingley. These exciting new collections are certain to make practicing more fun for young students, and piano lessons more rewarding for music teachers!

Though **Top Hits** correlates with *Alfred's Basic Piano Library*, the arrangements are so perfectly graded, they may be used to advantage with any piano method.

Level 1B (16496)
Casper the Friendly Ghost
Do-Re-Mi
Edelweiss
I'm Late
I'm Popeye the Sailor Man
It's a Small World
Mickey Mouse March
My Heart Will Go On
   (Love Theme from 'Titanic')
Peter Cottontail
Puff the Magic Dragon
Rubber Duckie

Level 2 (16497)
The Bare Necessities
Beauty and the Beast
Be Our Guest
Can You Feel the Love Tonight
The Grouch Song
My Favorite Things
Part of Your World
The Rainbow Connection
Supercalifragilisticexpialidocious
Tomorrow
What a Wonderful World
Won't You Be My Neighbor?

Level 3 (16498)
Colors of the Wind
Cruella De Vil
Heart and Soul
I Just Can't Wait to Be King
Memory
My Heart Will Go On
   (Love Theme from 'Titanic')
Nadia's Theme
Rockin' Robin
The Sound of Music
The Unbirthday Song
A Whole New World

Level 4 (16499)
The Addams Family Theme
Axel F
Beauty and the Beast
Can You Feel the Love Tonight
Chim Chim Cher-ee
Don't Cry for Me Argentina
It's the Hard-Knock Life
Mission: Impossible Theme
Think of Me
Under the Sea
Yesterday

 **Available now from your favorite music dealer.**

Published by
HAL•LEONARD CORPORATION